The Spanish Subjunctive Unleashed

Conquer Doubts and Hypotheticals with
Humor and Confidence

Carmen Gómez

To my wonderful students, who have faced the subjunctive with more questions than answers. This book is for those of you who have wished, hoped, and doubted your way through Spanish, learning that in both language and life, uncertainty isn't a barrier—it's an opportunity to grow and laugh along the way!

Copyright Page

© 2024 by Carmen Gomez. All rights reserved. No part of this book may be reproduced, distributed, or transmitted in any form or by any means, including photocopying, recording, or other electronic or mechanical methods, without the prior written permission of the publisher, except in the case of brief quotations used in critical reviews and certain other non-commercial uses permitted by copyright law.

Disclaimer

This book is intended to serve as an educational guide. While every effort has been made to ensure the accuracy of the information provided, the author and publisher assume no responsibility for errors or omissions, or for damages resulting from the use of the information contained herein.

The Mystery of the Subjunctive

The subjunctive mood in Spanish is often regarded as one of the most mysterious and challenging aspects of the language, but it's also one of the most powerful tools for expressing subtle nuances like hope, doubt, desire, and uncertainty. It is a world of possibility, where the speaker conveys not what is but what might be. In this chapter, we'll explore **why the subjunctive exists**, **how it plays a crucial role in everyday Spanish**, and **how it differs from the more familiar indicative mood**.

Why the Subjunctive?

The subjunctive exists to help speakers express uncertainty, desire, emotion, doubt, or hypothetical scenarios. Unlike the indicative mood, which deals with concrete facts and certainty, the subjunctive lives in the realm of possibilities, hopes, and things that may or may not come to pass.

For example, consider the difference between these two Spanish sentences:

- **Indicative:** *Yo sé que ella viene.* (I know that she is coming.)

- **Subjunctive:** *Espero que ella venga.* (I hope that she comes.)

The first sentence is a statement of fact—*ella viene* (she is coming)—indicating something that is certain or known to be true. This is the world of the **indicative** mood. In contrast, the second sentence expresses a hope or wish—*ella venga* (she comes)—something that may or may not happen. This is the domain of the **subjunctive** mood.

In many languages, like **English** or **German**, the subjunctive is not as prominent, and in everyday conversation, its usage has diminished over time. English, for example, mostly uses modal verbs like "may," "might," or "should" to express the same ideas conveyed by the subjunctive in Spanish.

- **English:** *I hope she comes.* (No explicit subjunctive form; "comes" remains the same as the indicative.)
- **German:** *Ich hoffe, dass sie kommt.* (Similar to English, with the indicative form of the verb.)

However, in languages like **Spanish** or **French**, the subjunctive is essential and frequently used in day-to-day communication. Compare the previous example to its French equivalent:

- **French:** *J'espère qu'elle vienne.* (I hope that she comes.)

In both Spanish and French, the verb changes to reflect the uncertainty or desire inherent in the sentence. This marks a significant difference from languages like English or German, where the subjunctive either isn't used at all or is much more limited.

In **Greek** and **Russian**, the subjunctive or similar moods exist but are used differently. In Greek, the **subjunctive** is more formalized and triggered in specific constructions:

- **Greek:** *Ελπίζω να έρθει.* (I hope that she comes.)

In this case, the subjunctive is triggered by the particle *να* and functions similarly to the Spanish construction. In **Russian**, however, speakers often rely on verb aspects and modal constructions to express ideas similar to the subjunctive:

- **Russian:** *Я надеюсь, что она придёт.* (I hope that she comes.)

In Russian, there's no specific verb form to indicate the subjunctive as there is in Spanish, but rather the meaning is conveyed through context and modality.

The Role of the Subjunctive in Everyday Spanish

While many learners first encounter the subjunctive in formal grammar lessons, its role in **everyday Spanish** cannot be overstated. Native speakers use the subjunctive frequently in regular conversations—often without even realizing it. The subjunctive mood is used in a wide variety of contexts, including:

- Expressing **wishes**: *Quiero que me ayudes.* (I want you to help me.)
- Indicating **doubt**: *Dudo que él venga.* (I doubt that he will come.)
- Conveying **emotions**: *Me alegra que estés aquí.* (I'm happy that you are here.)
- Stating **recommendations**: *Es importante que estudies.* (It's important that you study.)
- Making **requests**: *Te pido que vengas temprano.* (I ask that you come early.)

In these examples, the verbs *ayudes* (help), *venga* (come), *estés* (are), *estudies* (study), and *vengas* (come) are all in the subjunctive form, reflecting uncertainty, desire, or emotional nuance. These situations are part of everyday conversations where wishes, doubts, and emotions play a significant role.

In contrast, **indicative** mood is used for statements of fact, events that are seen as certain, and straightforward information:

- **Indicative:** *Sé que ella va al mercado.* (I know she is going to the market.)
- **Subjunctive:** *Espero que ella vaya al mercado.* (I hope she goes to the market.)

Here, the indicative *va* (goes) indicates certainty, while the subjunctive *vaya* (goes) reflects the speaker's hope or uncertainty about the event.

This distinction may not be as common in **English**, where we simply rely on modals or context to distinguish between certainty and doubt:

- **English Indicative:** *I know she is going to the market.*
- **English Subjunctive Equivalent:** *I hope she goes to the market.*

While both sentences use "goes" in English, the shift in meaning is conveyed through "I know" versus "I hope," without any changes in the verb itself.

The Subjunctive vs. The Indicative: What's the Difference?

The key difference between the subjunctive and the indicative is **certainty** versus **possibility**. The indicative deals with concrete facts, events, and descriptions of reality, while the subjunctive expresses ideas of doubt, uncertainty, wishes, or hypotheticals.

Indicative Mood:

The indicative is used when the speaker is certain about the information they are conveying. It is the mood of facts, descriptions, and real events.

- **Spanish (Indicative):** *Él viene mañana.* (He is coming tomorrow.)
- **English (Indicative):** *He is coming tomorrow.*

In both examples, the speaker is certain about the action: the person is coming tomorrow.

Subjunctive Mood:

The subjunctive is used when there is doubt, emotion, or subjectivity involved. It reflects the speaker's uncertainty or wish for something to happen.

- **Spanish (Subjunctive):** *Espero que él venga mañana.* (I hope he comes tomorrow.)

- **English (Subjunctive Equivalent):** *I hope he comes tomorrow.*

In these examples, there is no certainty that the person will come, only a hope or possibility.

Comparing to Other Languages:

- **French:** *Je veux qu'il vienne demain.* (I want him to come tomorrow.)
- **Greek:** *Θέλω να έρθει αύριο.* (I want him to come tomorrow.)
- **German:** *Ich will, dass er morgen kommt.* (I want him to come tomorrow.)

In all of these languages, there is a clear distinction between indicative certainty and subjunctive possibility. In contrast, **English** and **German** rely on context and word choice (like "hope" or "want") rather than specific verb forms, which are present in **Spanish**, **French**, and **Greek**.

Why Understanding the Subjunctive Is Essential

Mastering the subjunctive is crucial for truly grasping the nuances of the Spanish language. Unlike the indicative, which deals with concrete reality, the subjunctive allows speakers to express their feelings, doubts, and desires. It adds depth to conversation, allowing you to communicate uncertainty or possibility in a way that the indicative cannot.

In learning Spanish, recognizing when to use the subjunctive versus the indicative is key to sounding natural and fluent. The more you practice and become familiar with subjunctive triggers (such as emotions, doubts, and recommendations), the more comfortable and intuitive it will become.

Now, let's dive into the subjunctive mood itself and break down how it works, starting with the present subjunctive!

TABLE OF CONTENTS

Chapter 1: Understanding the Subjunctive Mood -- 1

Chapter 2: The Present Subjunctive ------ 12

Chapter 3: The Imperfect Subjunctive --- 23

Chapter 4: The Subjunctive in Everyday Conversations ----------------------------------- 35

Chapter 5: The Present Perfect Subjunctive -- 46

Chapter 6: The Pluperfect Subjunctive --- 57

Chapter 7: The Subjunctive vs. The Indicative: A Closer Look --------------------- 69

Chapter 8: The Subjunctive in Periphrasis Verbal Constructions --------------------------- 83

Chapter 9- : Mastering the Subjunctive with Practice -- 96

Chapter 10: Embracing Uncertainty with the Subjunctive -------------------------------- 107

Bibliography -------------------------------- *130*

Chapter 1

Understanding the Subjunctive Mood

"If life were always certain, the subjunctive wouldn't exist—thankfully, it does!"

The subjunctive mood is one of the most intriguing and essential aspects of the Spanish language. While it can be challenging for learners to grasp, it is an incredibly useful tool that allows speakers to express emotions, doubts, wishes, and hypothetical situations. In this chapter, we'll explore what the subjunctive is, when and why it's used, and how to structure it properly. We'll also provide bilingual examples and exercises to reinforce your understanding.

What Is the Subjunctive?

The subjunctive is a **mood** in Spanish that is used to express things that are uncertain, subjective, or not yet realized. Unlike the **indicative mood**, which deals with factual and concrete information (things that are real or known), the subjunctive operates in the world of possibilities, desires, doubts, and emotions. Think of the subjunctive as the language of "what if" and "I hope."

Example:

- **Indicative:** *Ella viene a la fiesta.* (She is coming to the party.)
- **Subjunctive:** *Espero que ella venga a la fiesta.* (I hope she comes to the party.)

Understanding the Subjunctive Mood

In the first sentence, the speaker knows for a fact that she is coming. It's a statement of reality, so the indicative mood is used. In the second sentence, the speaker is expressing a hope or wish, something that may or may not happen. Therefore, the verb switches to the subjunctive form.

In English, we don't have a fully developed subjunctive system like in Spanish, though we do use certain constructions to express similar ideas (using modal verbs like "might," "could," or "should"). For instance:

- **English Indicative: She is coming to the party.**
- **English Subjunctive Equivalent: I hope she comes to the party.**

However, in English, the verb form "comes" doesn't change like it would in Spanish. In **French** and **Italian**, like in Spanish, the subjunctive is more prominent and uses specific verb conjugations:

- **French:** *J'espère qu'elle vienne à la fête.* (I hope she comes to the party.)
- **Italian:** *Spero che lei venga alla festa.* (I hope she comes to the party.)

Both French and Italian employ distinct subjunctive verb forms, similar to Spanish.

When and Why the Subjunctive Is Used

The subjunctive in Spanish is triggered by a variety of situations that involve uncertainty, emotion, or subjectivity. Here are the most common situations where you'll need the subjunctive:

1. Wishes and Desires

Whenever you're expressing a hope, wish, or desire for something, the subjunctive is required.

Examples:

- **Espero que tengas un buen día.** (I hope you have a good day.)
- **Quiero que me llames más tarde.** (I want you to call me later.)

2. Doubt or Uncertainty

When you're expressing doubt or uncertainty about a situation, the subjunctive mood is used.

Examples:

- **Dudo que él venga a la reunión.** (I doubt that he will come to the meeting.)
- **No creo que esto sea cierto.** (I don't think this is true.)

Understanding the Subjunctive Mood

In contrast, the **indicative** mood would be used for statements of certainty:

- **Estoy seguro de que él viene a la reunión.** (I'm sure that he is coming to the meeting.)

In **English**, we often use modal verbs to express doubt or uncertainty, but we don't change the verb forms themselves as Spanish does:

- **English:** *I doubt he will come to the meeting.* (English does not require a specific verb change for the subjunctive.)

3. Emotions

The subjunctive is used when expressing emotions such as happiness, sadness, fear, or surprise about something uncertain.

Examples:

- **Me alegra que estés aquí.** (I'm glad that you are here.)
- **Temo que ellos no lleguen a tiempo.** (I'm afraid they won't arrive on time.)

4. Recommendations or Advice

When giving advice, recommendations, or commands in indirect speech, the subjunctive is also necessary.

Examples:

- **Es importante que estudies para el examen.** (It's important that you study for the exam.)
- **Te recomiendo que vayas al doctor.** (I recommend that you go to the doctor.)

5. Hypotheticals and Possibilities

In cases of hypotheticals, possibilities, or situations that may or may not happen, the subjunctive is used.

Examples:

- **Si tuviera más dinero, viajaría por el mundo.** (If I had more money, I would travel the world.)
- **Es posible que él no esté en casa.** (It's possible that he's not home.)

In **English**, we handle these situations with modal verbs like "might" or "could," but we don't change verb forms as much. In **German**, the **Konjunktiv** (subjunctive) mood is used in similar ways to Spanish:

- **German:** *Ich hoffe, dass er kommt.* (I hope that he comes.)
  (Here, the verb *kommt* stays in the same form as the indicative.)

Understanding the Subjunctive Mood

The Structure of the Subjunctive

Now that we've discussed when the subjunctive is used, let's look at how to form it. The **present subjunctive** is typically used in most of the contexts we've discussed so far, and it's fairly straightforward to form, even though many verbs are irregular.

Present Subjunctive Formation

1. **Start with the "yo" form of the present indicative.**
2. **Remove the -o ending.**
3. **Add the subjunctive endings** for the appropriate verb group (-ar, -er, -ir).

For **-ar** verbs, the subjunctive endings are:

- **Yo: -e**
- **Tú: -es**
- **Él/Ella/Usted: -e**
- **Nosotros: -emos**
- **Vosotros: -éis**
- **Ellos/Ellas/Ustedes: -en**

For **-er/-ir** verbs, the subjunctive endings are:

- **Yo: -a**

The Spanish Subjunctive Unleashed

- **Tú: -as**
- **Él/Ella/Usted: -a**
- **Nosotros: -amos**
- **Vosotros: -áis**
- **Ellos/Ellas/Ustedes: -an**

Example: Hablar (to speak)

- **Present Indicative (Yo):** *hablo*
- **Remove the -o → *habl-***
- **Add the subjunctive endings:**
  - Yo *hable*
  - Tú *hables*
  - Él/Ella/Usted *hable*
  - Nosotros *hablemos*
  - Vosotros *habléis*
  - Ellos/Ellas/Ustedes *hablen*

Example: Comer (to eat)

- **Present Indicative (Yo):** *como*
- **Remove the -o → *com-***
- **Add the subjunctive endings:**
- **Yo *coma***
  - Tú *comas*

- Él/Ella/Usted *coma*
- Nosotros *comamos*
- Vosotros *comáis*
- Ellos/Ellas/Ustedes *coman*

Examples & Exercises

Now, let's reinforce what we've learned with a few examples and exercises.

Examples

1. **Espero que tú estudies para el examen.**
   (I hope you study for the exam.)
2. **Dudo que él tenga suficiente dinero.**
   (I doubt that he has enough money.)
3. **Es importante que vayamos al médico.**
   (It's important that we go to the doctor.)
4. **Quiero que me llames esta noche.**
   (I want you to call me tonight.)

Exercises:

1. **Conjugation Practice:** Conjugate the following verbs in the present subjunctive form:

- *hablar* (to speak)
- *comer* (to eat)
- *vivir* (to live)

2. **Fill-in-the-Blank:** Complete the sentences with the correct form of the verb in the subjunctive:
   - Espero que tú ____ (venir) a la fiesta.
   - Dudo que ellos ____ (llegar) a tiempo.
   - Es importante que nosotros ____ (estudiar) más.

3. **Translation Practice:** Translate the following sentences into Spanish:
   - I want you to call me tomorrow.
   - It's possible that they are not home.
   - I hope we have good weather this weekend.

Understanding the Subjunctive

By now, you should have a clearer understanding of what the subjunctive mood is, when it's used, and how it differs from the indicative. The subjunctive is crucial for expressing doubt, emotion, and possibility in

Spanish, and while it may seem challenging at first, with practice, it will become second nature. Keep practicing the structures, and soon you'll be able to navigate the world of subjunctive sentences with confidence!

Chapter 2

The Present Subjunctive

"Wishing and hoping: The subjunctive's bread and butter!"

The Present Subjunctive

In this chapter, we dive into one of the most frequently used aspects of the subjunctive mood in Spanish—the **Present Subjunctive**. From expressing desires and doubts to giving recommendations, this mood is all about possibility and subjectivity. While it may seem tricky at first, the present subjunctive has clear patterns and rules you can master.

How to Form the Present Subjunctive

Forming the **present subjunctive** is straightforward once you know the formula. Whether regular or irregular, the process starts with the **"yo" form** of the **present indicative** (the "I" form). From there, you modify the endings for each pronoun.

Steps to Form the Present Subjunctive:

1. **Start with the first-person singular (yo) form of the present indicative.**
2. **Remove the "-o" ending.**
3. **Add the appropriate subjunctive endings** for the verb.

The Spanish Subjunctive Unleashed

Let's break this down by verb groups.

For -ar Verbs:

The endings for **-ar** verbs in the present subjunctive are:

- **Yo:** -e
- **Tú:** -es
- **Él/Ella/Usted:** -e
- **Nosotros:** -emos
- **Vosotros:** -éis
- **Ellos/Ellas/Ustedes:** -en

Example with hablar (to speak):

- **Present indicative (yo form)**: *hablo*
- **Remove the "o"**: *habl-*
- **Add the subjunctive endings**:
    - Yo **hable** (I speak)
    - Tú **hables** (You speak)
    - Él/Ella/Usted **hable** (He/She/You speak)
    - Nosotros **hablemos** (We speak)
    - Vosotros **habléis** (You all speak)
    - Ellos/Ellas/Ustedes **hablen** (They/You all speak)

The Present Subjunctive

For -er and -ir Verbs:

The endings for **-er** and **-ir** verbs are different from **-ar** verbs:

- **Yo**: -a
- **Tú**: -as
- **Él/Ella/Usted**: -a
- **Nosotros**: -amos
- **Vosotros**: -áis
- **Ellos/Ellas/Ustedes**: -an

Example with comer (to eat):

- **Present indicative (yo form)**: *como*
- **Remove the "o"**: *com-*
- **Add the subjunctive endings**:
    - Yo **coma** (I eat)
    - Tú **comas** (You eat)
    - Él/Ella/Usted **coma** (He/She/You eat)
    - Nosotros **comamos** (We eat)
    - Vosotros **comáis** (You all eat)
    - Ellos/Ellas/Ustedes **coman** (They/You all eat)

Key Irregular Verbs in the Present Subjunctive

While most verbs follow the regular pattern above, some important irregular verbs have unique forms in the subjunctive. These are often high-frequency verbs, so it's essential to learn them well.

1. Ser (to be)

Present Subjunctive:

- Yo **sea**
- Tú **seas**
- Él/Ella/Usted **sea**
- Nosotros **seamos**
- Vosotros **seáis**
- Ellos/Ellas/Ustedes **sean**

Example:

- **Espero que seas feliz.** (I hope that you are happy.)

2. Ir (to go)

Present Subjunctive:

- Yo **vaya**

The Present Subjunctive

- Tú **vayas**
- Él/Ella/Usted **vaya**
- Nosotros **vayamos**
- Vosotros **vayáis**
- Ellos/Ellas/Ustedes **vayan**

Example:

- **Es posible que vayamos al cine.** (It's possible that we will go to the cinema.)

3. Tener (to have)

Present Subjunctive:

- Yo **tenga**
- Tú **tengas**
- Él/Ella/Usted **tenga**
- Nosotros **tengamos**
- Vosotros **tengáis**
- Ellos/Ellas/Ustedes **tengan**

Example:

- **Espero que tengas un buen día.** (I hope you have a good day.)

4. Hacer (to do/make)

Present Subjunctive:

- Yo **haga**
- Tú **hagas**
- Él/Ella/Usted **haga**
- Nosotros **hagamos**
- Vosotros **hagáis**
- Ellos/Ellas/Ustedes **hagan**

Example:

- **Quiero que hagas tu tarea.** (I want you to do your homework.)

Comparing the Spanish Subjunctive to Other Languages

English:

English has a limited use of the subjunctive, often using modal verbs (like *may*, *might*, *should*) instead of changing verb forms. However, in formal contexts, there are remnants of the subjunctive in English.

The Present Subjunctive

Example:

- *I suggest that he **be** on time.*
  The verb *be* stays in the base form, unlike the usual *is* in indicative sentences. In modern spoken English, though, this construction is rare, and most speakers prefer using modal verbs.

French:

Like Spanish, French uses the subjunctive to express doubt, wishes, and uncertainty. The structure is similar, with specific conjugation changes.

French Example:

- *Il est important que tu **fasses** tes devoirs.* (It's important that you do your homework.)

Notice that, like in Spanish, the verb *faire* (to do) changes to *fasses* in the subjunctive form.

Chinese:

In **Mandarin Chinese**, there is no specific verb conjugation for different moods. Instead, speakers use particles or context to indicate subjunctive-like ideas. For example, 可能 (kěnéng) means "might" or "could," indicating possibility.

Example:

- *我可能去。* (Wǒ kěnéng qù.) – I might go.

While Chinese doesn't have a direct equivalent to the subjunctive, it uses words like *可能* to express uncertainty or possibility, achieving a similar effect without changing verb forms.

Arabic:

In **Arabic**, the **subjunctive mood** exists, particularly in Modern Standard Arabic, and is used after certain conjunctions to indicate wishes, conditions, or uncertainty.

Example:

- أرجو أن تذهب. (Arjū an tadhhaba.) – I hope you go.

Here, the verb *tadhhaba* (you go) is in the subjunctive mood because it follows the expression I hope.

Examples of the Present Subjunctive

1. **Espero que estudies para el examen.** *(I hope you study for the exam.)*

2. **Dudo que ella venga a tiempo.** *(I doubt that she will arrive on time.)*

3. **Es importante que nosotros hablemos con él.** *(It's important that we talk to him.)*

4. **Quiero que vayas al supermercado.** *(I want you to go to the supermarket.)*

Exercises

Exercise 1: Conjugation Practice

Conjugate the following verbs in the present subjunctive:

1. *hablar* (to speak)
2. *comer* (to eat)
3. *vivir* (to live)

Example Answer:

- *Hablar* → Yo **hable**, tú **hables**, él/ella/usted **hable**, nosotros **hablemos**, vosotros **habléis**, ellos/ellas/ustedes **hablen**.

Exercise 2: Fill in the Blanks

Complete the sentences with the correct form of the verb in parentheses, using the present subjunctive:

1. Quiero que tú ____ (venir) a la fiesta.
2. Dudo que ellos ____ (llegar) a tiempo.
3. Es posible que nosotros ____ (ir) al parque.
4. Espero que tú ____ (tener) un buen día.

Exercise 3: Translation Practice

Translate the following sentences into Spanish:

1. I hope that he eats early.
2. It's important that we study tonight.
3. I want you to speak with him.
4. I doubt that they will arrive on time.

Mastering the Present Subjunctive

The **present subjunctive** may feel challenging at first, but it plays an essential role in communicating desires, doubts, and possibilities in Spanish. By understanding its formation and practicing the most common irregular verbs, you'll be able to use it confidently in conversations.

Keep practicing, and soon the subjunctive will feel as natural as the indicative!

Chapter 3

The Imperfect Subjunctive

"Time traveling with the imperfect subjunctive:
Because even in the past, we doubted and dreamed!"

The **imperfect subjunctive** (or **past subjunctive**) allows us to express uncertainty, wishes, hypotheticals, and doubts about events that occurred in the past. It adds another layer of complexity to the Spanish subjunctive system, enabling speakers to refer to emotions, doubts, or desires from a past perspective.

In this chapter, we'll learn **how to form the imperfect subjunctive**, discuss **when it is used**, and provide **bilingual examples and exercises** to help solidify your understanding. Additionally, we will compare the use of the imperfect subjunctive in Spanish with other languages like English, French, and Arabic.

How to Form the Imperfect Subjunctive

The **imperfect subjunctive** has two different conjugation forms, but both are used interchangeably in modern Spanish: the **-ra** form and the less common **-se** form. For this chapter, we will focus on the **-ra** form, which is far more frequently used.

Steps to Form the Imperfect Subjunctive (with -ra endings):

The Imperfect Subjunctive

1. Start with the third-person plural (ellos/ellas/ustedes) form of the verb in the preterite tense.
2. Remove the -ron ending.
3. Add the imperfect subjunctive endings.

Imperfect Subjunctive Endings (-ra form):

For **-ar**, **-er**, and **-ir** verbs, the endings are the same:

- **Yo**: -ra
- **Tú**: -ras
- **Él/Ella/Usted**: -ra
- **Nosotros**: -ramos
- **Vosotros**: -rais
- **Ellos/Ellas/Ustedes**: -ran

Example: Hablar (to speak)

- **Third-person plural preterite form**: *hablaron*
- **Remove the -ron**: *habla-*
- **Add the imperfect subjunctive endings**:
  - Yo **hablara** (I spoke)
  - Tú **hablaras** (You spoke)

- Él/Ella/Usted **hablara** (He/She/You spoke)
- Nosotros **habláramos** (We spoke)
- Vosotros **hablarais** (You all spoke)
- Ellos/Ellas/Ustedes **hablaran** (They/You all spoke)

Example: Comer (to eat)

- **Third-person plural preterite form**: *comieron*
- **Remove the -ron**: *comie-*
- **Add the imperfect subjunctive endings**:
  - Yo **comiera** (I ate)
  - Tú **comieras** (You ate)
  - Él/Ella/Usted **comiera** (He/She/You ate)
  - Nosotros **comiéramos** (We ate)
  - Vosotros **comierais** (You all ate)
  - Ellos/Ellas/Ustedes **comieran** (They/You all ate)

Example: Vivir (to live)

- **Third-person plural preterite form**: *vivieron*
- **Remove the -ron**: *vivie-*

- **Add the imperfect subjunctive endings**:
  - Yo **viviera** (I lived)
  - Tú **vivieras** (You lived)
  - Él/Ella/Usted **viviera** (He/She/You lived)
  - Nosotros **viviéramos** (We lived)
  - Vosotros **vivierais** (You all lived)
  - Ellos/Ellas/Ustedes **vivieran** (They/You all lived)

When to Use the Imperfect Subjunctive

The **imperfect subjunctive** is used in specific scenarios where the action being discussed occurred in the past, but the mood still expresses doubt, uncertainty, emotion, desire, or a hypothetical situation. There are several common contexts where the imperfect subjunctive is required:

1. When the main clause is in the past tense

If the main clause is in the preterite, imperfect, or conditional tenses, and the subordinate clause requires the subjunctive, we use the imperfect subjunctive.

Examples:

- **Querìa que él viniera a la fiesta.** *(I wanted him to come to the party.)*

    Here, *quería* (I wanted) is in the past, so the verb in the subordinate clause *viniera* (to come) is in the imperfect subjunctive.

- **Esperaba que ellos pudieran ayudarme.** *(I was hoping that they could help me.)*

2. After certain conjunctions that require the subjunctive

Like in the present subjunctive, conjunctions such as *aunque* (even though), *a menos que* (unless), and *antes de que* (before) trigger the imperfect subjunctive when referring to past events.

Examples:

- **Lo hice antes de que ellos llegaran.**
  (I did it before they arrived.)
- **Salimos aunque lloviera.**
  (We left even though it was raining.)

3. Hypotheticals in the past (with "if" clauses)

The imperfect subjunctive is essential when talking about hypothetical situations in the past using the conjunction *si* (if).

The Imperfect Subjunctive

Examples:

- **Si tuviera más dinero, viajaría por todo el mundo.**
  (If I had more money, I would travel around the world.)
- **Si ellos estudiaran más, sacarían mejores notas.**
  (If they studied more, they would get better grades.)

4. Politeness in requests or suggestions

In Spanish, the imperfect subjunctive is often used to make polite requests or suggestions.

Examples:

- **Quisiera hablar contigo.**
  (I would like to speak with you.)
- **Me gustaría que me ayudara.**
  (I would like you to help me.)

Comparing the Imperfect Subjunctive in Spanish to Other Languages

The subjunctive mood is not unique to Spanish. Many other languages, such as **French**, **Italian**, and **Portuguese**, have a similar system, while some languages, like **English** and **Chinese**, express these ideas differently.

English:

English does not have a fully developed subjunctive system, especially for past events. Instead, we rely heavily on modal verbs like "would," "could," or "might" to convey uncertainty or hypotheticals.

Example:

- *If I had more money, I would travel.*
  In English, "had" and "would travel" convey the same hypothetical meaning as the Spanish sentence *Si tuviera más dinero, viajaría.*

French:

Like Spanish, **French** uses the imperfect subjunctive, but it's much less common in modern spoken French. The equivalent of the Spanish imperfect subjunctive is the **subjonctif imparfait**, which is mostly found in literary texts.

Example in French:

- *Je voulais qu'il vînt à la fête.*
  (I wanted him to come to the party.)

The Imperfect Subjunctive

In French, the **subjonctif imparfait** (*vînt*) mirrors the Spanish *viniera*, but this form is rarely used in everyday conversation.

Arabic:

Modern Standard Arabic (MSA) uses a form similar to the imperfect subjunctive in conditional clauses. However, the usage is not as widespread in spoken dialects.

Example in Arabic:

- لو كان لديّ المال، لسافرت.
  (If I had the money, I would travel.)

Here, had and would travel are used to express a past hypothetical, much like Spanish's *tuviera* and *viajaría*.

Chinese:

In **Mandarin Chinese**, there isn't an equivalent verb conjugation system to mark the subjunctive mood. Instead, speakers use auxiliary words and context to express hypotheticals or wishes.

Example in Mandarin:

- *如果我有更多*钱，*我会去旅行*。
  (If I had more money, I would travel.)

In this sentence, 如果 (rúguǒ) means "if," and 会 (huì) acts as a marker of possibility, conveying a similar hypothetical meaning to the Spanish imperfect subjunctive.

Examples & Exercises

1. **Quería que me llamaras ayer.**
   (I wanted you to call me yesterday.)

2. **Si tuviera tiempo, iría contigo.**
   (If I had time, I would go with you.)

3. **Esperaba que pudieras venir.**
   (I was hoping you could come.)

4. **Ojalá que ellos estuvieran aquí.**
   (I wish they were here.)

Exercises

Exercise 1: Conjugation Practice

Conjugate the following verbs in the **imperfect subjunctive**:

1. *hablar* (to speak)
2. *comer* (to eat)

3. *vivir* (to live)

Exercise 2: Fill in the Blanks

Complete the following sentences with the correct form of the verb in the imperfect subjunctive:

1. **Quería que tú ____ (venir) a la fiesta.**
2. **Si ellos ____ (tener) dinero, viajarían más.**
3. **Me gustaría que tú ____ (ayudarme) con esto.**
4. **Esperaba que nosotros ____ (poder) salir esta noche.**

Exercise 3: Translation Practice

Translate the following sentences into Spanish using the imperfect subjunctive:

1. I wished that he had more time.
2. If I knew the answer, I would tell you.
3. I hoped that they would come to the meeting.
4. It was important that we studied for the exam.

Mastering the Imperfect Subjunctive

The **imperfect subjunctive** opens the door to expressing doubts, desires, and hypothetical situations from the past. Though it requires practice, understanding this mood will enrich your Spanish conversations and give you greater flexibility to talk about complex past scenarios.

Keep practicing with the exercises and examples, and soon the imperfect subjunctive will become second nature in your Spanish toolkit!

Chapter 4

The Subjunctive in Everyday Conversations

"Where there's uncertainty, there's the subjunctive—especially in daily life!"

The **subjunctive mood** in Spanish isn't just for lofty literary works or formal writing—it's an essential part of **everyday conversations**. Whether you're expressing doubts, desires, or uncertainty about the future, the subjunctive is ever-present in how native speakers communicate. Once you get comfortable with it, you'll find that the subjunctive makes your speech more nuanced and fluid.

In this chapter, we'll explore **common phrases and expressions** that trigger the subjunctive, dive into how the subjunctive is used to express **hopes, desires, and doubts**, and provide **bilingual examples and exercises** to help you practice its usage in everyday conversations. We'll also take a look at how other languages handle these situations, comparing Spanish with **English**, **French**, **Arabic**, and **Mandarin Chinese**.

Common Phrases and Expressions Triggering the Subjunctive

In Spanish, certain phrases and expressions naturally trigger the use of the subjunctive. These phrases are often used to express uncertainty, emotion, possibility,

The Subjunctive in Everyday Conversations

or subjectivity. When you encounter these expressions, it's a clear signal to switch into the subjunctive mood.

1. Expressions of Doubt or Uncertainty

When there's doubt or uncertainty about whether something is true or will happen, the subjunctive is required. This is different from the indicative mood, which is used for statements of certainty or fact.

Common Phrases:

- **Dudo que** (I doubt that)
- **No creo que** (I don't believe that)
- **Es posible que** (It's possible that)
- **No es seguro que** (It's not certain that)
- **No pienso que** (I don't think that)

Examples:

- **Dudo que él venga.** (I doubt that he's coming.)
- **No creo que haya terminado.** (I don't think he has finished.)
- **Es posible que llueva mañana.** (It's possible that it will rain tomorrow.)

In **English**, we don't have a full subjunctive system like in Spanish, but we express uncertainty through **modal verbs** like "might," "may," and "could."

English Example:

- *I doubt that he is coming.*
  (No verb form change, but doubt is expressed through context.)

In **French**, the **subjunctive mood** is also triggered by similar expressions of doubt:

French Example:

- *Je doute qu'il vienne.* (I doubt that he's coming.)

---

2. Expressions of Emotion

When emotions like happiness, sadness, surprise, or regret are involved, the subjunctive is used in the dependent clause. These phrases indicate that the speaker's emotions depend on an outcome that may not be certain.

Common Phrases:

- **Me alegra que** (I'm happy that)
- **Siento que** (I'm sorry that)

The Subjunctive in Everyday Conversations

- **Me sorprende que** (I'm surprised that)
- **Temo que** (I'm afraid that)

Examples:

- **Me alegra que estés aquí.** (I'm happy that you are here.)
- **Siento que no puedas venir.** (I'm sorry that you can't come.)
- **Me sorprende que hayan terminado tan rápido.** (I'm surprised that they finished so quickly.)

In **English**, we generally express emotion using regular verb structures, without requiring a change in verb form. However, in more formal or old-fashioned English, the **subjunctive** still appears in certain constructions, though it is quite rare today.

English Example:

- *I'm happy that you are here.*

In **French**, emotions also trigger the subjunctive mood in a similar way:

French Example:

- *Je suis heureux que tu sois ici.* (I'm happy that you are here.)

3. Expressions of Desire or Wishes

When you express a wish or desire for something to happen, it triggers the subjunctive. The outcome of the wish is uncertain, so the subjunctive mood is required.

Common Phrases:

- **Espero que** (I hope that)
- **Quiero que** (I want that)
- **Ojalá que** (Hopefully/If only)
- **Prefiero que** (I prefer that)

Examples:

- **Espero que tengas un buen día.** (I hope you have a good day.)
- **Quiero que me llames mañana.** (I want you to call me tomorrow.)
- **Ojalá que no llueva.** (Hopefully, it won't rain.)
- **Prefiero que comas antes de salir.** (I prefer that you eat before leaving.)

In **Arabic**, the **subjunctive mood** is used to express wishes or desires in certain formal contexts, though spoken dialects vary. In **Classical Arabic** and **Modern Standard Arabic**, the subjunctive follows verbs of desire:

Arabic Example:

The Subjunctive in Everyday Conversations

- أتمنى أن يأتي. *(Atamanna an ya'ti.)* (I hope that he comes.)

In **Mandarin Chinese**, there is no distinct subjunctive mood, but the speaker expresses desires using particles or auxiliary verbs that suggest possibility or wish.

Chinese Example:

- *我希望你能来。* *(Wǒ xīwàng nǐ néng lái.)* (I hope you can come.)

The Subjunctive with Hopes, Desires, and Doubts

Let's take a deeper look at how the subjunctive is used when discussing hopes, desires, and doubts in Spanish. These three concepts are at the heart of the subjunctive mood and appear in countless everyday conversations.

Hopes:

When expressing a hope or wish for the future, the subjunctive is essential. The key here is that the outcome is uncertain or not yet realized.

Example Sentences:

- **Espero que puedas venir a la fiesta.**
  (I hope that you can come to the party.)
- **Ojalá que no haya tráfico.**
  (Hopefully, there won't be any traffic.)

Desires:

When you want or prefer something to happen, but it's not guaranteed, you must use the subjunctive.

Example Sentences:

- **Quiero que tú estudies más.**
  (I want you to study more.)
- **Prefiero que cenemos temprano.**
  (I prefer that we have dinner early.)

Doubts:

When you are unsure or doubt something, it's a clear sign to use the subjunctive.

Example Sentences:

- **No creo que ellos entiendan la situación.**
  (I don't think they understand the situation.)
- **Dudo que ella llegue a tiempo.**
  (I doubt that she will arrive on time.)

In comparison, **English** handles doubt and desire through auxiliary verbs or modals rather than through verb conjugation, making the subjunctive far less visible.

Examples & Exercises

Let's apply what we've learned so far with examples and exercises. Practicing these will help you become more comfortable using the subjunctive in real-life conversations.

Examples

1. **Quiero que me llames mañana.**
   (I want you to call me tomorrow.)

2. **No creo que él tenga tiempo hoy.**
   (I don't think he has time today.)

3. **Me alegra que estés aquí.**
   (I'm happy that you are here.)

4. **Dudo que ellos vengan al evento.**
   (I doubt that they will come to the event.)

5. **Espero que tengas un buen viaje.**
   (I hope you have a good trip.)

Exercises

Exercise 1: Conjugation Practice

Conjugate the following verbs in the present subjunctive to match the context of the sentence.

1. **Quiero que tú ____ (venir) a la reunión.**
2. **No creo que ella ____ (tener) tiempo.**
3. **Me sorprende que ellos ____ (llegar) tan temprano.**
4. **Espero que ustedes ____ (hacer) la tarea.**

Exercise 2: Fill in the Blanks

Fill in the blanks with the appropriate verb form in the subjunctive:

1. **Dudo que ellos ____ (poder) asistir a la boda.**
2. **Es posible que nosotros ____ (salir) esta noche.**
3. **Ojalá que no ____ (llover) mañana.**
4. **Me alegra que tú ____ (estar) de acuerdo conmigo.**

The Subjunctive in Everyday Conversations

Exercise 3: Translation Practice

Translate the following sentences into Spanish:

1. I hope that she can come tomorrow.
2. I doubt that they will understand the instructions.
3. I want you to bring the book to class.
4. It's possible that we will see each other next week.

The Subjunctive in Daily Life

As you can see, the **subjunctive** is deeply embedded in daily Spanish conversations. It's not just for formal or hypothetical situations; it's there when we express our wishes, doubts, and emotions. While other languages like **English** rely more on modals or context, Spanish speakers frequently switch to the subjunctive to convey uncertainty or subjectivity.

The more you practice, the more natural it will feel to use the subjunctive, helping you to sound more fluent and expressive in everyday interactions!

Chapter 5

The Present Perfect Subjunctive

"It's never too late to doubt what could have been!"

The Present Perfect Subjunctive

The **present perfect subjunctive** is a powerful tool in Spanish for expressing uncertainty, doubt, or emotion about events that have already occurred. While the present subjunctive deals with the present or future, the present perfect subjunctive allows you to bring this doubt or uncertainty into the past. In this chapter, we'll cover how to form the present perfect subjunctive, when and why it's used, and provide bilingual examples and exercises to practice. Additionally, we'll compare this tense with how similar concepts are handled in languages like **English**, **French**, and **Portuguese**.

How to Form the Present Perfect Subjunctive

The present perfect subjunctive (in Spanish, **pretérito perfecto del subjuntivo**) is formed by combining two elements:

1. **The present subjunctive of the verb "haber"** (to have, as an auxiliary verb).
2. **The past participle** of the main verb.

Present Subjunctive of "haber":

- **Yo**: haya

- **Tú**: hayas
- **Él/Ella/Usted**: haya
- **Nosotros**: hayamos
- **Vosotros**: hayáis
- **Ellos/Ellas/Ustedes**: hayan

Past Participles:

The **past participle** is formed by taking the infinitive form of the verb and adding **-ado** for **-ar** verbs and **-ido** for **-er/-ir** verbs. For irregular verbs, the past participle varies (like "escrito" for "escribir" or "visto" for "ver").

Examples of Past Participles:

- *hablar* → **hablado** (spoken)
- *comer* → **comido** (eaten)
- *vivir* → **vivido** (lived)
- *hacer* → **hecho** (done)
- *escribir* → **escrito** (written)

Formation Example:

To form the **present perfect subjunctive**, combine the subjunctive form of "haber" with the past participle of the main verb.

The Present Perfect Subjunctive

Example with hablar:

- **Yo haya hablado** (I have spoken)
- **Tú hayas hablado** (You have spoken)
- **Él/Ella/Usted haya hablado** (He/She/You have spoken)
- **Nosotros hayamos hablado** (We have spoken)
- **Vosotros hayáis hablado** (You all have spoken)
- **Ellos/Ellas/Ustedes hayan hablado** (They/You all have spoken)

When and Why It's Used

The **present perfect subjunctive** is used in situations where the speaker is expressing doubt, emotion, or subjectivity about actions or events that have **already happened**. It's frequently used in **dependent clauses** when the main clause indicates uncertainty or a feeling about a past event.

When to Use the Present Perfect Subjunctive:

1. **When expressing emotion, doubt, or hope about past events:**

The Spanish Subjunctive Unleashed

- The speaker is unsure about something that happened in the past or has feelings about it.

Examples:

- **Me alegra que hayas venido.** (I'm glad that you have come.)
- **Dudo que él haya terminado el proyecto.** (I doubt that he has finished the project.)

2. **When the main clause is in the present, but the action in the subordinate clause is in the past:**

   - The main clause refers to the present or future, but the action you're unsure about, hoping for, or reacting to, is in the past.

   Examples:

   - **Es posible que hayan visto la película.** (It's possible that they have seen the movie.)
   - **No creo que haya hecho la tarea.** (I don't think he has done the homework.)

3. **When talking about something that "could have been":**

The Present Perfect Subjunctive

- This is often used in hypothetical or unreal scenarios, when discussing something that might have happened but you're unsure or it didn't happen.

Examples:

- **Espero que lo hayas entendido.** (I hope that you have understood it.)

- **Ojalá que hayamos hecho lo correcto.** (Hopefully, we have done the right thing.)

Comparison to Other Languages:

- **English:** In English, the **present perfect subjunctive** is not explicitly marked like in Spanish. Instead, we use modal verbs (may/might have) along with the **present perfect** to express similar ideas of doubt or uncertainty about past events.

Examples:

- *I doubt that he has finished the project.*

- *It's possible that they have seen the movie.*

Here, English maintains the **present perfect** form but adds modals like "may" or "might" for uncertainty, instead of changing the verb itself.

- **French:** The **subjunctive passé composé** in French functions similarly to the present perfect subjunctive in Spanish. It is formed by using the **subjunctive form of "avoir" or "être"** followed by the **past participle** of the main verb.

    Example in French:

    - *Je doute qu'il ait terminé le projet. (I doubt that he has finished the project.)*

Like Spanish, French keeps the subjunctive mood for past events that involve doubt or uncertainty.

- **Portuguese:** In **Portuguese**, the present perfect subjunctive, **pretérito perfeito do subjuntivo**, mirrors Spanish in both form and function.

    Example in Portuguese:

    - *Espero que você tenha feito o trabalho. (I hope that you have done the work.)*

Similar to Spanish, Portuguese uses the subjunctive form of **ter** (to have) followed by the past participle to form this tense.

- **Arabic:** In **Arabic**, there is no direct equivalent to the present perfect subjunctive.

Instead, speakers rely on different verb structures and particles to express doubts or emotions about past events. The past tense and imperfect forms can be used with specific conjunctions to achieve a similar meaning.

Examples of the Present Perfect Subjunctive

Let's take a look at some bilingual examples of how the present perfect subjunctive is used in Spanish to express doubt, emotion, or uncertainty about past events.

1. **No creo que ella haya comido.**
   (I don't think she has eaten.)

2. **Me sorprende que hayas terminado tan rápido.**
   (I'm surprised that you have finished so quickly.)

3. **Es posible que ellos hayan salido temprano.**
   (It's possible that they have left early.)

4. **Ojalá que hayamos hecho lo correcto.**
   (Hopefully, we have done the right thing.)

5. **Dudo que hayan visto la película.**
   (I doubt that they have seen the movie.)

Exercises

Exercise 1: Conjugation Practice

Conjugate the following verbs in the present perfect subjunctive for the indicated subject.

1. **Hablar** (to speak) – **Nosotros**
2. **Comer** (to eat) – **Tú**
3. **Vivir** (to live) – **Ellos**
4. **Escribir** (to write) – **Yo**
5. **Hacer** (to do/make) – **Ella**

Exercise 2: Fill in the Blanks

Complete the sentences with the correct form of the present perfect subjunctive.

1. Me alegra que tú ____ (comer) bien.
2. No creo que ellos ____ (ver) la noticia.
3. Dudo que él ____ (hacer) su tarea.
4. Es posible que nosotros ____ (terminar) el trabajo.
5. Espero que ustedes ____ (entender) la lección.

The Present Perfect Subjunctive

Exercise 3: Translation Practice

Translate the following sentences into Spanish using the present perfect subjunctive.

1. I doubt that he has finished the project.
2. I'm glad that you have come to the meeting.
3. It's possible that they have gone to the store.
4. Hopefully, we have passed the exam.
5. I don't think they have read the book.

Mastering the Present Perfect Subjunctive

The **present perfect subjunctive** allows us to express uncertainty, emotion, or doubt about past actions in Spanish. It brings depth to our conversations, enabling us to reflect on what may or may not have occurred. While other languages, such as English, French, and Portuguese, handle similar scenarios with different structures, the present perfect subjunctive is a core part of Spanish grammar. By practicing the conjugation and applying it in real-life situations, you'll soon feel comfortable using this form to express complex ideas with ease.

The Spanish Subjunctive Unleashed

Keep practicing and you'll see how naturally it fits into everyday conversations!

Chapter 6

The Pluperfect Subjunctive

"If only I had known the pluperfect subjunctive earlier..."

The **pluperfect subjunctive** (also known as **past perfect subjunctive**) is one of the more advanced tenses in Spanish, but it's extremely useful when you want to express hypothetical situations or doubts about something that **could have** or **should have happened** in the past. It's the perfect tool for reflecting on those what-if scenarios and missed opportunities that we all ponder from time to time. In this chapter, we'll learn how to form the pluperfect subjunctive, when and why it's used, and how it compares to other languages. Finally, we'll practice using the tense with bilingual examples and exercises.

How to Form the Pluperfect Subjunctive

The **pluperfect subjunctive** is formed by combining two elements:

1. The **imperfect subjunctive** form of the verb **haber** (to have, as an auxiliary verb).
2. The **past participle** of the main verb.

Imperfect Subjunctive of Haber:

- **Yo**: hubiera / hubiese
- **Tú**: hubieras / hubieses
- **Él/Ella/Usted**: hubiera / hubiese

The Pluperfect Subjunctive

- **Nosotros**: hubiéramos / hubiésemos
- **Vosotros**: hubierais / hubieseis
- **Ellos/Ellas/Ustedes**: hubieran / hubiesen

Both **hubiera** and **hubiese** are used interchangeably. The **hubiera** form is more common in modern Spanish, while **hubiese** is more formal and often found in literary or older texts.

Past Participles:

As with other perfect tenses, the past participle is used. For regular verbs, the past participle is formed by adding **-ado** for **-ar** verbs and **-ido** for **-er** and **-ir** verbs. Irregular verbs have unique past participle forms (e.g., *escribir → escrito; ver → visto*).

Examples:

- *hablar* → **hablado** (spoken)
- *comer* → **comido** (eaten)
- *vivir* → **vivido** (lived)
- *hacer* → **hecho** (done)

Formation Example:

To form the **pluperfect subjunctive**, combine the imperfect subjunctive form of *haber* with the past participle of the main verb.

Example with hablar (to speak):

- **Yo hubiera hablado** (I would have spoken)
- **Tú hubieras hablado** (You would have spoken)
- **Él/Ella/Usted hubiera hablado** (He/She/You would have spoken)
- **Nosotros hubiéramos hablado** (We would have spoken)
- **Vosotros hubierais hablado** (You all would have spoken)
- **Ellos/Ellas/Ustedes hubieran hablado** (They would have spoken)

Example with hacer (to do/make):

- **Yo hubiera hecho** (I would have done)
- **Tú hubieras hecho** (You would have done)
- **Él/Ella/Usted hubiera hecho** (He/She/You would have done)
- **Nosotros hubiéramos hecho** (We would have done)
- **Vosotros hubierais hecho** (You all would have done)
- **Ellos/Ellas/Ustedes hubieran hecho** (They would have done)

The What-If Scenarios of the Past

The **pluperfect subjunctive** is primarily used in Spanish to talk about hypothetical or counterfactual situations in the past—what we often call **"what-if" scenarios**. These are events or actions that didn't actually happen but could have happened under different circumstances. This makes the pluperfect subjunctive a great tool for expressing **regret**, **wishes**, **hypothetical outcomes**, and **uncertainty** about the past.

Common Uses:

1. **Conditional Sentences (with "if")** The pluperfect subjunctive is often used in **third conditional sentences**, where we express what might have happened if the past had been different. These sentences use the pluperfect subjunctive in the **if-clause** and the conditional perfect in the result clause.

   Examples:
   - **Si hubiera sabido la respuesta, te la habría dicho.**
     (If I had known the answer, I would have told you.)

- **Si hubieras llegado a tiempo, no habríamos perdido el tren.**
  (If you had arrived on time, we wouldn't have missed the train.)

2. **Wishes About the Past** The pluperfect subjunctive is used with expressions like **ojalá** (if only, I wish) to express wishes or regrets about things that didn't happen in the past.

Examples:

- **Ojalá hubiera estudiado más.**
  (If only I had studied more.)
- **Ojalá no hubiera llovido ayer.**
  (If only it hadn't rained yesterday.)

3. **Doubt, Emotion, or Uncertainty About Past Actions** It's used when we express emotions, doubts, or uncertainty about past actions in a subordinate clause, especially when the main clause is in the present or imperfect.

Examples:

- **Dudaba que ellos hubieran terminado el proyecto.**
  (I doubted that they had finished the project.)
- **Me sorprendió que hubieras llegado tan temprano.**

(I was surprised that you had arrived so early.)

Comparing the Pluperfect Subjunctive in Other Languages

While the **pluperfect subjunctive** in Spanish has no exact equivalent in many languages, other languages have ways of expressing similar past hypotheticals and counterfactuals, though the structures may differ significantly.

English:

In English, we typically use the **past perfect** along with modal verbs like **would have**, **could have**, or **should have** to express past hypotheticals. English does not have a distinct pluperfect subjunctive form like Spanish, but the meaning is often the same.

Examples:

- *If I had known the answer, I would have told you.*
  (Si hubiera sabido la respuesta, te la habría dicho.)
- *I wish I had studied more.*
  (Ojalá hubiera estudiado más.)

In English, we rely on **would have** and **had** constructions, while in Spanish, the pluperfect subjunctive serves this purpose in a single verb structure.

French:

French uses the **plus-que-parfait du subjonctif** (pluperfect subjunctive), though it's very rare in modern French and mostly appears in formal writing. Instead, most French speakers use the **past conditional** or **plus-que-parfait de l'indicatif** to express past hypotheticals.

French Example:

- *Si j'avais su la réponse, je te l'aurais dite.*
  (If I had known the answer, I would have told you.)

This structure is closer to the **pluperfect indicative** in Spanish, though the meaning and usage are very similar.

Portuguese:

Portuguese, like Spanish, has a **pluperfect subjunctive** known as **pretérito mais-que-perfeito do subjuntivo**. It functions almost identically to its Spanish counterpart, expressing past hypotheticals and counterfactuals.

The Pluperfect Subjunctive

Portuguese Example:

- *Se eu tivesse sabido a resposta, teria te dito.*
  (If I had known the answer, I would have told you.)

Arabic:

In **Modern Standard Arabic**, there is no direct equivalent to the pluperfect subjunctive. Instead, past hypothetical scenarios are expressed using combinations of past tense verbs and conditional particles. This often requires context or auxiliary verbs to express the same meaning.

Arabic Example:

- لو كنت قد عرفت الجواب، لكنت أخبرتك.
  (If I had known the answer, I would have told you.)

Examples & Exercises

Examples

1. **Si hubieras estudiado más, habrías pasado el examen.**
   (If you had studied more, you would have passed the exam.)

2. **Ojalá hubiéramos visto esa película antes.**
   (If only we had seen that movie earlier.)

3. **Me sorprendió que hubieras terminado tan rápido.**
   (I was surprised that you had finished so quickly.)

4. **Si ellos hubieran llegado a tiempo, habríamos comenzado la reunión.**
   (If they had arrived on time, we would have started the meeting.)

Exercises

Exercise 1: Conjugation Practice

Conjugate the following verbs in the pluperfect subjunctive for the given subject:

1. *hablar* (to speak) – **Yo**
2. *comer* (to eat) – **Nosotros**
3. *vivir* (to live) – **Ellos**
4. *escribir* (to write) – **Tú**
5. *hacer* (to do/make) – **Ella**

Exercise 2: Fill in the Blanks

The Pluperfect Subjunctive

Fill in the blanks with the correct form of the pluperfect subjunctive:

1. Si tú ____ (comer) antes, no habrías tenido hambre.
2. Ojalá ____ (ir) con ellos al concierto.
3. Me habría alegrado si tú ____ (venir) a la fiesta.
4. No creo que ellos ____ (terminar) el proyecto a tiempo.
5. Si nosotros ____ (saber) la verdad, habríamos actuado de otra manera.

Exercise 3: Translation Practice

Translate the following sentences into Spanish using the pluperfect subjunctive:

1. If I had known about the meeting, I would have attended.
2. I wish they had told me the truth.
3. If she had studied more, she would have passed the exam.
4. I doubt that they had finished before the deadline.
5. If only we had met earlier.

Embracing the Pluperfect Subjunctive

Mastering the **pluperfect subjunctive** allows you to delve into those hypothetical and counterfactual scenarios that so often populate our conversations. It gives you the ability to express regret, wishes, and doubts about past events with nuance and precision. While other languages, like **English** and **French**, use different structures to express these ideas, the pluperfect subjunctive is a cornerstone of Spanish grammar, and its proper use will make your Spanish sound more advanced and sophisticated. Keep practicing, and soon you'll be able to navigate these complex structures with ease!

Chapter 7

The Subjunctive vs. The Indicative: A Closer Look

"Why does the subjunctive have to complicate things? Because life isn't always factual!"

The **subjunctive** and **indicative** moods represent two different ways of approaching reality in Spanish. The **indicative** is the realm of facts, certainties, and objective truths, while the **subjunctive** deals with subjectivity, doubt, uncertainty, and emotions. Understanding when to use each mood is one of the key challenges for learners of Spanish, but mastering this distinction will greatly improve your fluency and natural expression.

In this chapter, we'll take a closer look at how to distinguish between the subjunctive and the indicative, explore the key triggers and clues that tell you which mood to use, and compare the usage of these moods with other languages like **English**, **French**, **Portuguese**, and **Arabic**.

Understanding When to Use the Subjunctive or the Indicative

The **indicative mood** is used to describe actions, events, or states that are seen as real, certain, or objective. The **subjunctive mood**, on the other hand, is used when the speaker expresses uncertainty, subjectivity, emotion, desire, or doubt about the action or event.

The Subjunctive vs. The Indicative: A Closer Look

When to Use the Indicative:

The indicative is used for:

1. **Statements of fact**: Things that are known to be true.
   - **Example:** *Ella está aquí.* (She is here.)
2. **Descriptions**: Objective descriptions of people, places, or things.
   - **Example:** *La casa es grande.* (The house is big.)
3. **Actions that are certain**: Things that have definitely happened, are happening, or will happen.
   - **Example:** *Voy al cine mañana.* (I'm going to the movies tomorrow.)
4. **Beliefs**: When there's no doubt about the speaker's belief.
   - **Example:** *Sé que él está estudiando.* (I know that he is studying.)

When to Use the Subjunctive:

The subjunctive is used when the speaker expresses uncertainty, emotion, or subjectivity. It's often used in dependent clauses following certain verbs or conjunctions that trigger the subjunctive.

1. **Doubt and Uncertainty**: The action is not certain.
   - **Example:** *Dudo que él venga a la fiesta.* (I doubt that he is coming to the party.)

2. **Emotion**: The action or event triggers an emotional response.
   - **Example:** *Me alegra que estés aquí.* (I'm glad that you are here.)
3. **Wishes and Desires**: The speaker wants something to happen, but it's not guaranteed.
   - **Example:** *Quiero que tú estudies más.* (I want you to study more.)
4. **Possibility or Hypotheticals**: When discussing what might or might not happen.
   - **Example:** *Es posible que vayamos al parque mañana.* (It's possible that we'll go to the park tomorrow.)
5. **Recommendations and Advice**: Making suggestions or giving advice.
   - **Example:** *Es importante que descanses.* (It's important that you rest.)

In **English**, there is no formal subjunctive system like in Spanish, but we use modal verbs (like "might," "could," or "should") to convey similar meanings. **For example:**

- **English Indicative:** *I know that she is coming to the party.*

The Subjunctive vs. The Indicative: A Closer Look

- **English Subjunctive Equivalent:** *I doubt that she is coming to the party.*

In the English example above, there's no distinct change in verb form between the indicative and subjunctive clauses. Instead, the mood is implied through the context or auxiliary verbs.

Key Triggers and Clues for Using the Subjunctive

The **subjunctive mood** is not randomly used in Spanish. Certain verbs, expressions, and conjunctions reliably trigger the use of the subjunctive in the dependent clause. Let's look at the most common **triggers** for the subjunctive and some **clues** to help you identify when it should be used.

1. Verbs of Doubt, Denial, or Uncertainty

When the main verb expresses doubt, denial, or uncertainty about the action in the dependent clause, the subjunctive is required.

Examples:

- **Dudar que** (to doubt that): *Dudo que él venga a la fiesta.* (I doubt that he is coming to the party.)

- **No creer que** (not to believe that): *No creo que ella sepa la verdad.* (I don't believe that she knows the truth.)
- **Negar que** (to deny that): *Niegan que hayan robado algo.* (They deny that they have stolen anything.)

2. Verbs of Emotion or Feeling

When the main verb expresses an emotion or feeling about the action in the dependent clause, the subjunctive is needed.

Examples:

- **Alegrarse de que** (to be happy that): *Me alegra que estés aquí.* (I'm glad that you are here.)
- **Temer que** (to fear that): *Temo que no podamos terminar a tiempo.* (I fear that we won't be able to finish on time.)
- **Sorprenderse de que** (to be surprised that): *Me sorprende que él haya llegado tan temprano.* (I'm surprised that he arrived so early.)

3. Verbs of Wanting, Wishing, or Desiring

The Subjunctive vs. The Indicative: A Closer Look

When the main verb expresses a wish or desire for the future or an action that may or may not happen, the subjunctive is required in the dependent clause.

Examples:

- **Querer que** (to want that): *Quiero que tú vengas mañana.* (I want you to come tomorrow.)
- **Esperar que** (to hope that): *Espero que puedas asistir al evento.* (I hope that you can attend the event.)
- **Preferir que** (to prefer that): *Prefiero que ella lo haga.* (I prefer that she does it.)

4. Conjunctions that Trigger the Subjunctive

Certain conjunctions always trigger the use of the subjunctive in the clause that follows them, especially those that introduce conditions, purposes, or time constraints.

Common Conjunctions:

- **Para que** (so that): *Voy a salir temprano para que no lleguemos tarde.* (I'm going to leave early so that we don't arrive late.)

- **A menos que** (unless): *No saldré a menos que dejes de llover.* (I won't go out unless it stops raining.)
- **Antes de que** (before): *Lávate las manos antes de que comas.* (Wash your hands before you eat.)

5. Impersonal Expressions

Certain impersonal expressions that express opinions, possibilities, or uncertainties trigger the subjunctive.

Examples:

- **Es posible que** (It's possible that): *Es posible que él llegue tarde.* (It's possible that he'll arrive late.)
- **Es importante que** (It's important that): *Es importante que estudies para el examen.* (It's important that you study for the exam.)
- **Es necesario que** (It's necessary that): *Es necesario que ellos lo terminen hoy.* (It's necessary that they finish it today.)

Examples of the Subjunctive vs. Indicative

Let's look at some bilingual examples that contrast the **subjunctive** and **indicative** moods. In each case, the

The Subjunctive vs. The Indicative: A Closer Look

subjunctive is triggered by uncertainty, emotion, or subjectivity, while the indicative is used for certainty and facts.

1. **Indicative:** *Sé que Juan está en casa.*
   (I know that Juan is at home.)
   Subjunctive: *No creo que Juan esté en casa.*
   (I don't think that Juan is at home.)

2. **Indicative:** *Ella trabaja en el banco.*
   (She works at the bank.)
   Subjunctive: *Es posible que ella trabaje en el banco.*
   (It's possible that she works at the bank.)

3. **Indicative:** *Es cierto que él viene a la fiesta.*
   (It's certain that he is coming to the party.)
   Subjunctive: *Dudo que él venga a la fiesta.*
   (I doubt that he is coming to the party.)

Comparing Subjunctive Use in Other Languages

English:

While English doesn't have a full subjunctive system like Spanish, it still retains some forms, especially in formal or old-fashioned expressions. English often relies on modal verbs like **may**, **might**, **could**, or **should** to express doubt, emotion, or possibility.

- **English Example (Subjunctive):**
  I suggest that he be on time.
  (Subjunctive form "be" instead of "is.")

- **English Example (Modal Verb):**
  It's possible that he might be late.

French:

In **French**, the **subjunctive mood** is also used in similar contexts as in Spanish, triggered by doubt, emotion, or uncertainty. French verbs conjugate differently depending on whether they're in the **indicative** or **subjunctive** mood.

- **French Indicative:** *Je sais qu'il vient.*
  (I know that he is coming.)

- **French Subjunctive:** *Je doute qu'il vienne.*
  (I doubt that he is coming.)

Portuguese:

In **Portuguese**, the subjunctive is used similarly to Spanish, particularly after expressions of doubt, emotion, or uncertainty.

The Subjunctive vs. The Indicative: A Closer Look

- **Portuguese Indicative:** *Eu sei que ele está aqui.*
  (I know that he is here.)

- **Portuguese Subjunctive:** *Eu duvido que ele esteja aqui.*
  (I doubt that he is here.)

Arabic:

Modern Standard Arabic also uses mood to indicate doubt or certainty. Subjunctive-like forms are often expressed through the **jussive mood**, which is used in conditional and volitional clauses.

- **Arabic Example:**
  أن أعتقد *(A'taqidu annahu)*
  (I think that...) triggers the indicative.
  أن أخشى *(Akhsha annahu)*
  (I fear that...) triggers the subjunctive-like jussive.

Exercises

Exercise 1: Identifying the Subjunctive or Indicative

For each sentence below, decide whether the verb in the dependent clause should be in the **indicative** or **subjunctive**.

1. **Sé que** ella (venir) mañana.
2. **Dudo que** tú (tener) razón.
3. **Es posible que** nosotros (salir) tarde.
4. **Estoy seguro de que** ellos (saber) la respuesta.
5. **No creo que** él (hacer) el trabajo.

Exercise 2: Fill in the Blanks

Complete the sentences with the correct form of the verb in either the subjunctive or indicative.

1. No pienso que ella ____ (hablar) con él.
2. Creo que nosotros ____ (poder) hacerlo mañana.
3. Es importante que tú ____ (comer) bien antes del examen.
4. Sé que tú ____ (tener) razón.

The Subjunctive vs. The Indicative: A Closer Look

5. Dudo que ellos ____ (comprender) la situación.

Exercise 3: Translation Practice

Translate the following sentences into Spanish, using either the indicative or subjunctive as appropriate.

1. I'm sure that he is coming to the meeting.
2. I doubt that she has finished her homework.
3. It's possible that we'll go to the park tomorrow.
4. I don't believe that they are telling the truth.
5. I'm happy that you are here.

Mastering the Subjunctive and Indicative

The distinction between the **subjunctive** and **indicative** moods is essential for fluent and nuanced communication in Spanish. While the **indicative** covers statements of fact, certainty, and reality, the **subjunctive** delves into the world of doubt, emotion, possibility, and subjectivity. As you continue practicing and applying the key triggers and clues, using the subjunctive will become second nature. By comparing with other languages, you'll see that while

Spanish makes this distinction more explicit, the underlying concepts are universal!

Keep practicing, and soon you'll master both moods with ease!

Chapter 8

The Subjunctive in Periphrasis Verbal Constructions

"Because two verbs are better than one when you're doubting the future!"

The subjunctive mood is already complex on its own, but when you add periphrasis—two or more verbs working together—it gets even more interesting. **Periphrasis** occurs when you combine an auxiliary or modal verb with another verb to express a nuanced meaning. In Spanish, periphrastic constructions often combine the **subjunctive mood** with irregular verbs to express desires, doubts, emotions, or uncertainties, especially regarding future actions.

In this chapter, we'll explore how to use **irregular verbs** in the subjunctive with periphrastic constructions, common phrases that trigger the subjunctive in these contexts, and how Spanish compares to other languages in handling such structures. By the end, you'll see why "two verbs are better than one" in making your Spanish more expressive.

Using Irregular Verbs with the Subjunctive

The **subjunctive mood** in periphrastic constructions often involves irregular verbs, which means you'll need to be familiar with their specific forms. Irregular verbs in the **subjunctive** don't follow regular conjugation

The Subjunctive in Periphrasis Verbal Constructions

patterns, making them a bit tricky, but mastering these will significantly improve your fluency.

Let's review the subjunctive forms of a few key **irregular verbs** that often appear in periphrastic constructions:

Ir (to go):

- **Yo vaya**
- **Tú vayas**
- **Él/Ella/Usted vaya**
- **Nosotros vayamos**
- **Vosotros vayáis**
- **Ellos/Ellas/Ustedes vayan**

Example in a periphrasis:

- **Quiero que vayas al médico.**
  (I want you to go to the doctor.)

Tener (to have):

- **Yo tenga**
- **Tú tengas**
- **Él/Ella/Usted tenga**
- **Nosotros tengamos**
- **Vosotros tengáis**

- **Ellos/Ellas/Ustedes tengan**

Example in a periphrasis:

- **Es importante que tengas tiempo para descansar.**
  (It's important that you have time to rest.)

Hacer (to do/make):

- **Yo haga**
- **Tú hagas**
- **Él/Ella/Usted haga**
- **Nosotros hagamos**
- **Vosotros hagáis**
- **Ellos/Ellas/Ustedes hagan**

Example in a periphrasis:

- **Prefiero que él haga los arreglos.**
  (I prefer that he makes the arrangements.)

Common Subjunctive Periphrastic Constructions

In Spanish, periphrastic constructions combine two or more verbs to express complex ideas, often involving uncertainty, doubt, or desire. When the main verb expresses a subjective idea (doubt, desire, emotion, etc.), the second verb in the periphrasis usually appears in the **subjunctive** mood.

1. Expressions of Desire or Recommendation

When one person wants, suggests, or requires something from another, the subjunctive is triggered in the second verb. These expressions often use irregular verbs, and they are essential for giving advice, making requests, or expressing personal desires.

Examples:

- **Quiero que** + subjunctive:
  Quiero que tú vengas mañana.
  (I want you to come tomorrow.)

- **Prefiero que** + subjunctive:
  Prefiero que él haga el trabajo.
  (I prefer that he does the work.)

- **Es necesario que** + subjunctive:
  Es necesario que nosotros estudiemos más.
  (It's necessary that we study more.)

2. Expressions of Doubt or Uncertainty

Verbs and expressions that indicate doubt or uncertainty require the subjunctive in the second verb of the periphrastic construction. This is common when someone is unsure about the future or about someone's actions.

Examples:

- **Dudo que** + subjunctive:
  Dudo que él pueda venir a la reunión.
  (I doubt that he can come to the meeting.)

- **No creo que** + subjunctive:
  No creo que ellos lleguen a tiempo.
  (I don't think they'll arrive on time.)

- **Es posible que** + subjunctive:
  Es posible que vayamos al cine esta noche.
  (It's possible that we'll go to the cinema tonight.)

3. Expressions of Emotion

When the main verb expresses an emotional response to something, the subjunctive is required in the dependent clause. These expressions convey feelings such as happiness, sadness, fear, or surprise about someone's actions.

Examples:

- **Me alegra que** + subjunctive:
  Me alegra que hayas venido.
  (I'm glad that you came.)

The Subjunctive in Periphrasis Verbal Constructions

- **Temo que** + subjunctive:
  Temo que no podamos terminar a tiempo.
  (I'm afraid that we won't be able to finish on time.)

- **Me sorprende que** + subjunctive:
  Me sorprende que ellos hayan terminado tan rápido.
  (I'm surprised that they finished so quickly.)

4. Conjunctions that Trigger the Subjunctive

Certain conjunctions, particularly those that indicate purpose, condition, or time, require the subjunctive in the second verb of the periphrastic construction.

Examples:

- **Para que** + subjunctive:
  Salgo temprano para que no lleguemos tarde.
  (I'm leaving early so that we don't arrive late.)

- **A menos que** + subjunctive:
  No saldremos a menos que deje de llover.
  (We won't go out unless it stops raining.)

- **Antes de que** + subjunctive:
  Lávate las manos antes de que comas.
  (Wash your hands before you eat.)

Comparing Subjunctive Periphrasis in Other Languages

Periphrasis and the subjunctive mood exist in various languages, though the specifics vary. Let's compare how periphrastic constructions work in Spanish with other languages like **English**, **French**, **Portuguese**, and **Arabic**.

English:

In **English**, periphrastic constructions are common, but the subjunctive is not explicitly marked as it is in Spanish. Instead, English uses modal verbs like **may**, **might**, or **should** to express doubt, desire, or recommendation. The second verb remains in its base form without conjugation changes.

Example in English:

- *I want you to go to the doctor.*
  (No verb form change, but the meaning is subjective.)//
- *It's important that he do his homework.*
  (Here, "do" remains in the base form, expressing the subjunctive mood, though this is rare in modern English.)

The Subjunctive in Periphrasis Verbal Constructions

French:

In **French**, the **subjunctive mood** is used similarly to Spanish, often in periphrastic constructions where the main verb expresses doubt, emotion, or necessity. French, like Spanish, requires the second verb to be in the subjunctive.

Examples in French:

- *Je veux que tu fasses tes devoirs.*
  (I want you to do your homework.)
- *Il est important que vous soyez là.*
  (It's important that you be there.)

Portuguese:

Portuguese has a subjunctive system that is nearly identical to Spanish in both form and function. In periphrastic constructions, Portuguese uses the subjunctive in the second verb when expressing emotions, desires, doubts, or hypotheticals.

Examples in Portuguese:

- *Espero que você vá ao médico.*
  (I hope that you go to the doctor.)
- *É importante que ele faça o trabalho.*
  (It's important that he does the work.)

Arabic:

In **Modern Standard Arabic**, there is no exact equivalent of the subjunctive mood as in Spanish, but periphrastic constructions exist, and certain particles trigger specific verb forms. For example, when expressing desire or purpose, the **jussive mood** or verbs in conditional constructions are used.

Example in Arabic:

- الطبيب إلى تذهب أن أريد *(Urid an tadhhaba ila attabeeb)*
  (I want you to go to the doctor.)
  (The particle *an* triggers the subjunctive-like form *tadhhaba*.)

Examples of Subjunctive Periphrasis

Let's look at some bilingual examples of how periphrastic constructions work in Spanish, focusing on the subjunctive in each case.

1. **Quiero que tú vengas mañana.**
   (I want you to come tomorrow.)

2. **Es importante que estudies para el examen.**
   (It's important that you study for the exam.)

3. **Dudo que ellos puedan terminar a tiempo.**
   (I doubt that they can finish on time.)

The Subjunctive in Periphrasis Verbal Constructions

4. **Me sorprende que hayas hecho todo el trabajo.**
   (I'm surprised that you've done all the work.)

5. **Vamos a salir temprano para que no lleguemos tarde.**
   (We're going to leave early so that we don't arrive late.)

Exercises

Exercise 1: Conjugation Practice

Conjugate the following verbs in the subjunctive for the given subject and periphrastic construction.

1. *hacer* (to do) – **Yo quiero que tú...**
2. *venir* (to come) – **Es importante que él...**
3. *salir* (to leave) – **Prefiero que nosotros...**
4. *hablar* (to speak) – **Dudo que ellos...**

Exercise 2: Fill in the Blanks

Complete the sentences with the correct form of the verb in the subjunctive.

1. **Quiero que tú ____ (comer) antes de salir.**
2. **Es posible que nosotros ____ (ver) una película esta noche.**

3. **Dudo que ella _____ (hacer) el trabajo a tiempo.**
4. **Espero que ellos _____ (poder) venir a la reunión.**

Exercise 3: Translation Practice

Translate the following sentences into Spanish, using periphrastic constructions with the subjunctive.

1. I want you to finish the project before the deadline.
2. It's important that they be on time for the meeting.
3. I doubt that she can come to the party.
4. We need to leave early so that we don't miss the train.

The Power of Periphrasis with the Subjunctive

Mastering **periphrasis** with the **subjunctive mood** in Spanish allows you to express complex ideas about doubt, desire, and uncertainty. By combining two verbs, you can make your language more nuanced and precise. While other languages, such as English and French, handle periphrasis differently, the underlying

The Subjunctive in Periphrasis Verbal Constructions

goal of expressing subjectivity remains the same. Practice these constructions, and soon you'll find that using two verbs is, indeed, better than one when navigating the complexities of future possibilities!

Chapter 9

Mastering the Subjunctive with Practice

"It's not about perfection—it's about practicing until you feel confident!"

Mastering the **subjunctive** in Spanish is not a matter of overnight perfection; it's a journey that requires practice and patience. The more you practice, the more natural the subjunctive will feel. By reinforcing key concepts with exercises and comparing how other languages handle similar structures, you will solidify your understanding of the subjunctive mood. In this chapter, we'll provide a variety of exercises and bilingual examples to help you build confidence in using the subjunctive, while also drawing comparisons with languages like **English**, **French**, **Portuguese**, and **Arabic**.

Exercises to Reinforce the Subjunctive

The subjunctive in Spanish is used in a variety of contexts: expressing doubt, emotions, uncertainty, desires, and hypotheticals. To reinforce these ideas, you need to practice regularly with both written and spoken exercises.

Let's break down key areas of the subjunctive and reinforce them with exercises.

1. Subjunctive for Expressing Doubt or Uncertainty

When expressing doubt or uncertainty, the subjunctive is mandatory in the subordinate clause.

Examples:

- **Dudo que ella venga a la fiesta.**
  (I doubt that she's coming to the party.)

- **No creo que ellos sepan la respuesta.**
  (I don't believe they know the answer.)

In **English**, doubt is expressed using modal verbs like "might" or "could," but the verb form remains the same.

English Comparison:

- *I doubt that she is coming to the party.*
  (No verb change, but "doubt" is expressed through context.)

In **French**, doubt also triggers the subjunctive.

French Example:

- *Je doute qu'elle vienne à la fête.*
  (I doubt that she's coming to the party.)

Mastering the Subjunctive with Practice

Exercise 1: Complete the Sentence with the Subjunctive

Fill in the blanks with the correct subjunctive form of the verb.

1. **Dudo que tú ____ (saber) la respuesta.**
2. **No creo que ellos ____ (venir) a tiempo.**
3. **Es posible que nosotros ____ (tener) que esperar.**

---

2. Subjunctive for Expressing Emotions

The subjunctive is triggered when the main clause expresses an emotional reaction to the action of the subordinate clause. This is true for happiness, sadness, surprise, fear, and more.

Examples:

- **Me alegra que estés aquí.**
  (I'm glad that you are here.)
- **Temo que no podamos salir esta noche.**
  (I'm afraid that we won't be able to go out tonight.)

In **English**, emotions are expressed without a change in verb form. However, the subjunctive can be implied through context.

English Example:

- *I'm glad that you are here.*
  (No subjunctive form, but the emotion is conveyed.)

In **Portuguese**, emotional reactions similarly trigger the subjunctive.

Portuguese Example:

- *Estou feliz que você esteja aqui.*
  (I'm happy that you are here.)

Exercise 2: Choose the Correct Verb

Fill in the sentence with the appropriate form of the verb in the subjunctive.

1. **Me sorprende que tú ____ (hablar) tan bien español.**
2. **Temo que él no ____ (poder) hacerlo solo.**
3. **Estoy contento de que ellos ____ (venir) a la reunión.**

3. Subjunctive for Expressing Desires and Recommendations

When expressing wishes, desires, or recommendations, the subjunctive must be used in the dependent clause. This includes verbs like **querer** (to want), **esperar** (to hope), and **recomendar** (to recommend).

Examples:

- **Quiero que tú estudies más.**
  (I want you to study more.)

- **Es importante que ellos lleguen a tiempo.**
  (It's important that they arrive on time.)

In **English**, we typically express desires with the base form of the verb, but we don't change the verb to a specific subjunctive form.

English Comparison:

- *I want you to study more.*
  (No subjunctive conjugation required.)

In **French**, desires trigger the subjunctive as well.

French Example:

- *Je veux que tu étudies plus.*
  (I want you to study more.)

Exercise 3: Expressing Wishes or Desires

Translate the following sentences into Spanish using the subjunctive mood.

1. I hope that you finish the project.
2. It's important that they arrive early.
3. I want you to do the homework.

---

4. Subjunctive in Hypotheticals and Uncertainty

The subjunctive is frequently used in **hypothetical situations**—scenarios that are uncertain or unreal. This often includes sentences with **if** (si), where the action is contrary to reality or expresses doubt.

Examples:

- **Si yo fuera tú, hablaría con ella.**
  (If I were you, I would talk to her.)

- **Es posible que vayamos al cine esta noche.**
  (It's possible that we'll go to the movies tonight.)

In **English**, hypotheticals are expressed with modal verbs like "would" or "could," but the verb form remains unchanged.

English Example:

Mastering the Subjunctive with Practice

- *If I were you, I would talk to her.*

In **Arabic**, hypotheticals and conditional sentences often use specific particles to indicate that the action is unreal or uncertain.

Arabic Example:

- معها لتحدثت ،مكانك كنت لو *(Law kunt makanak, latahaddathu ma'aha)*
  (If I were you, I would talk to her.)

Exercise 4: Hypotheticals in the Subjunctive

Complete the following sentences with the correct form of the verb in the subjunctive.

1. **Si yo ____ (tener) más tiempo, iría al gimnasio.**
2. **Es posible que nosotros ____ (ver) esa película mañana.**
3. **Si ellos ____ (ser) más responsables, habrían terminado a tiempo.**

---

5. Subjunctive with Conjunctions

Certain **conjunctions** in Spanish always trigger the subjunctive because they introduce conditions, purposes, or time limits. These include conjunctions like **para que** (so that), **a menos que** (unless), and **antes de que** (before).

Examples:

- **Voy a salir temprano para que no lleguemos tarde.**
  (I'm going to leave early so that we don't arrive late.)

- **A menos que deje de llover, no saldremos.**
  (Unless it stops raining, we won't go out.)

In **English**, conjunctions like "so that" or "unless" don't trigger a change in the verb, but the meaning remains similar.

English Example:

- *I'm leaving early so that we don't arrive late.*

In **Portuguese**, these conjunctions trigger the subjunctive, just like in Spanish.

Portuguese Example:

- *Vou sair cedo para que não cheguemos tarde.*
  (I'm going to leave early so that we don't arrive late.)

Exercise 5: Using Subjunctive with Conjunctions

Complete the sentences using the correct form of the subjunctive.

1. **Voy a hablar con él antes de que ____ (salir).**
2. **Saldré a menos que ____ (llover).**
3. **Es importante que nosotros ____ (estudiar) antes del examen.**

The Key to Mastering the Subjunctive is Practice

The **subjunctive** mood is one of the most challenging aspects of Spanish, but through consistent practice, it becomes a natural part of your language skills. By working through the exercises in this chapter and focusing on key triggers—such as doubt, emotion, desire, and hypotheticals—you will steadily build confidence. Comparing the subjunctive to how other languages handle similar situations will help you understand that while Spanish makes the subjunctive explicit, other languages express these ideas through different structures.

Remember, it's not about perfection, but about practicing until you feel comfortable using the subjunctive in everyday conversations!

Keep practicing, and you'll find that this once daunting mood becomes second nature in your Spanish toolkit.

Chapter 10

Embracing Uncertainty with the Subjunctive

"The subjunctive is like a surprise party—it's always lurking around the corner, but once you get the hang of it, you'll start enjoying the excitement!"

The subjunctive mood, often seen as a challenge for language learners, is actually one of the most fascinating and expressive parts of the Spanish language. As we wrap up this journey through the subjunctive, it's time to reflect on how far you've come, the uncertainty you've mastered, and how this mood can now become a natural part of your conversations.

The Subjunctive Is Your Friend (Really!)

At the beginning of this journey, the subjunctive may have felt like a mystery. Its rules, triggers, and irregularities seemed like hurdles to overcome. However, as you've worked through each chapter, you've come to realize that the subjunctive is not an enemy—it's a powerful tool that enriches your Spanish. The subjunctive allows you to express emotions, desires, doubts, and hypothetical situations in ways that the **indicative** just can't.

Instead of focusing solely on memorizing conjugations, you've learned to recognize the **why** behind the subjunctive. It's about subjectivity and possibility, about expressing **what could be** rather than what **is**. Understanding this key difference will help you see that the subjunctive is your ally, allowing you to communicate more naturally and fluently.

Let's Recap the Key Takeaways:

- The **subjunctive mood** is triggered when there is **uncertainty, emotion, doubt, desire, or hypothetical scenarios**.

- Many verbs, phrases, and conjunctions naturally trigger the subjunctive, such as **"quiero que"**, **"es posible que"**, and **"antes de que"**.

- Irregular verbs in the subjunctive follow their own patterns, but with practice, they become second nature.

- **Periphrasis**, or the combination of two verbs to express more complex ideas, often involves the subjunctive when dealing with recommendations, emotions, or conditions.

By understanding when and why to use the subjunctive, you've moved beyond simple memorization and into **real communication**. The subjunctive gives you the tools to express nuanced feelings, possibilities, and conditions that define much of human interaction. It's not about making your language more complicated—it's about making your communication **richer**.

Encouragement for Your Spanish Journey

As you continue your journey toward mastering Spanish, remember that the subjunctive is just one piece of the puzzle. Learning any language, especially one as expressive and nuanced as Spanish, is a long-term process. The subjunctive, though initially challenging, is a milestone in your path toward fluency.

Tips to Continue Building Your Subjunctive Skills:

1. **Immerse Yourself in Spanish**
   The more you hear and see the subjunctive in action, the easier it will be to use it naturally. Watch Spanish movies, listen to Spanish music or podcasts, and read Spanish books. Pay attention to how native speakers use the subjunctive in their everyday speech.

2. **Practice Through Conversation**
   One of the best ways to cement your knowledge is through practice. Try engaging in conversation with native speakers or language exchange partners where you focus on using the subjunctive in real-time situations. Don't worry about making mistakes—every conversation helps you get better!

3. **Keep a Journal in Spanish**
   Journaling is a great way to apply what you've learned. Write about your day, your hopes,

your doubts, and your emotions—all while using the subjunctive where appropriate. For example: *Espero que mañana haga sol* (I hope that tomorrow it's sunny).

4. **Review and Reflect**
   Language learning is never linear. Take the time to review past lessons and reflect on how far you've come. Practice subjunctive constructions that still give you trouble and celebrate the ones you've mastered.

5. **Stay Curious**
   Language is a living, evolving thing, and Spanish is no different. Stay curious and continue learning new ways to use the subjunctive. Don't be afraid to ask questions and explore new contexts where the subjunctive might appear.

Final Thoughts and Next Steps

Mastering the subjunctive is one of the biggest leaps you'll take in learning Spanish, but it's not the end of the journey. Spanish, like all languages, is rich with depth, and the more you learn, the more you'll discover. As you become more comfortable with the subjunctive, you'll notice that you can express yourself with more **confidence, precision, and flair**.

Keep practicing and embracing the subjunctive, because it's not just about understanding grammar rules—it's about being able to navigate the **uncertainties of life** in another language. You'll find that Spanish becomes more personal and intuitive the more you use it.

Next Steps in Your Spanish Learning Journey:

1. **Expand Your Vocabulary**
   Now that you're comfortable with the subjunctive, start expanding your vocabulary to enrich your conversations. Learn more idiomatic expressions, explore colloquial phrases, and dive deeper into specific topics that interest you.

2. **Explore Other Complex Tenses**
   While the subjunctive is challenging, Spanish has other complex tenses worth exploring, such as the **future perfect** or the **conditional perfect**. These tenses will help you communicate even more effectively about past and future events.

3. **Engage with Native Speakers**
   The ultimate goal of language learning is communication. Whether it's through online language exchanges, travel, or in-person conversation, immerse yourself in the

language and engage with native speakers whenever possible. The more you speak, the more natural your use of the subjunctive will become.

4. **Stay Motivated**
   Language learning is a marathon, not a sprint. Celebrate the progress you've made, but keep your eyes on the road ahead. Use your love for the language, its culture, and its people to fuel your continued learning.

Embrace the Subjunctive, Embrace Spanish

In conclusion, the **subjunctive** isn't just a grammatical tool; it's a way of thinking. It allows you to express hopes, doubts, desires, and uncertainties—concepts that define much of human experience. By mastering the subjunctive, you're not just becoming more fluent in Spanish—you're opening yourself up to a richer way of expressing yourself.

So, embrace the subjunctive. Use it confidently in your conversations. Allow it to help you navigate the uncertainties of life, whether you're speaking about the past, present, or future.

¡**Buena suerte** (Good luck) on the rest of your Spanish journey, and remember: **It's not about perfection— it's about practice and progress!**

Exercises and Answers

Chapter 1: Understanding the Subjunctive Mood

Exercise 1: Complete the Sentence with the Subjunctive

Fill in the blanks with the correct form of the verb in the subjunctive.

1. Dudo que tú **sepas** (saber) la respuesta.
2. No creo que ellos **vengan** (venir) a tiempo.
3. Es posible que nosotros **tengamos** (tener) que esperar.

Exercise 2: Choose the Correct Verb

Fill in the sentence with the appropriate form of the verb in the subjunctive.

1. Me sorprende que tú **hables** (hablar) tan bien español.
2. Temo que él no **pueda** (poder) hacerlo solo.
3. Estoy contento de que ellos **vengan** (venir) a la reunión.

Exercise 3: Translation Practice

Translate the following sentences into Spanish using the subjunctive mood.

1. I doubt that she will come to the party.
   Dudo que ella venga a la fiesta.
2. I hope that you finish the project.
   Espero que termines el proyecto.
3. It's important that they arrive early.
   Es importante que ellos lleguen temprano.

Chapter 2: The Present Subjunctive

Exercise 1: Conjugation Practice

Conjugate the following verbs in the present subjunctive.

1. *Hablar* (to speak) – **Yo hable**
2. *Comer* (to eat) – **Tú comas**
3. *Escribir* (to write) – **Él escriba**
4. *Vivir* (to live) – **Nosotros vivamos**
5. *Ver* (to see) – **Ellos vean**

Exercise 2: Fill in the Blanks

Fill in the blanks with the correct present subjunctive verb form.

1. No creo que ella **pueda** (poder) venir hoy.
2. Es posible que tú **estudies** (estudiar) más tarde.
3. Espero que nosotros **hablemos** (hablar) pronto.
4. Me alegra que ellos **vivan** (vivir) cerca.

Exercise 3: Translation Practice

Translate the following sentences into Spanish using the present subjunctive.

1. I want you to come to the meeting.
   Quiero que tú vengas a la reunión.

2. It's possible that we'll go to the park.
   Es posible que vayamos al parque.

3. I hope that he speaks with her.
   Espero que él hable con ella.

Chapter 3: The Imperfect Subjunctive

Exercise 1: Conjugation Practice

Conjugate the following verbs in the imperfect subjunctive.

1. *Tener* (to have) – **Yo tuviera**
2. *Ser* (to be) – **Tú fueras**
3. *Ir* (to go) – **Él fuera**
4. *Hacer* (to do/make) – **Nosotros hiciéramos**
5. *Poder* (to be able) – **Ellos pudieran**

Exercise 2: Fill in the Blanks

Complete the following sentences with the correct form of the verb in the imperfect subjunctive.

1. Quería que tú **vinieras** (venir) a la fiesta.

2. Si ellos **tuvieran** (tener) dinero, viajarían más.

3. Me gustaría que tú **me ayudaras** (ayudarme) con esto.

4. Esperaba que nosotros **pudiéramos** (poder) salir esta noche.

Exercise 3: Translation Practice

Translate the following sentences into Spanish using the imperfect subjunctive.

1. I wished that he had more time.
   Deseaba que él tuviera más tiempo.

2. If I knew the answer, I would tell you.
   Si yo supiera la respuesta, te la diría.

3. I hoped that they would come to the meeting.
   Esperaba que ellos vinieran a la reunión.

4. It was important that we studied for the exam.
   Era importante que estudiáramos para el examen.

Chapter 4: The Present Perfect Subjunctive

Exercise 1: Conjugation Practice

Conjugate the following verbs in the present perfect subjunctive.

1. *Hablar* (to speak) – **Nosotros hayamos hablado**
2. *Comer* (to eat) – **Tú hayas comido**
3. *Vivir* (to live) – **Ellos hayan vivido**
4. *Escribir* (to write) – **Yo haya escrito**
5. *Hacer* (to do/make) – **Ella haya hecho**

Exercise 2: Fill in the Blanks

Fill in the blanks with the correct form of the present perfect subjunctive.

1. Me alegra que tú **hayas comido** (comer) bien.
2. No creo que ellos **hayan visto** (ver) la noticia.
3. Dudo que él **haya hecho** (hacer) su tarea.
4. Es posible que nosotros **hayamos terminado** (terminar) el trabajo.

Exercise 3: Translation Practice

Translate the following sentences into Spanish using the present perfect subjunctive.

1. I doubt that he has finished the project.
   Dudo que él haya terminado el proyecto.
2. I'm glad that you have come to the meeting.
   Me alegra que hayas venido a la reunión.

3. It's possible that they have gone to the store.
   Es posible que ellos hayan ido a la tienda.

4. Hopefully, we have passed the exam.
   Ojalá que hayamos pasado el examen.

Chapter 5: The Pluperfect Subjunctive

Exercise 1: Conjugation Practice

Conjugate the following verbs in the pluperfect subjunctive.

1. *Hablar* (to speak) – **Yo hubiera hablado**
2. *Comer* (to eat) – **Nosotros hubiéramos comido**
3. *Vivir* (to live) – **Ellos hubieran vivido**
4. *Escribir* (to write) – **Tú hubieras escrito**
5. *Hacer* (to do/make) – **Ella hubiera hecho**

Exercise 2: Fill in the Blanks

Complete the sentences with the correct form of the pluperfect subjunctive.

1. Si tú **hubieras comido** (comer) antes, no habrías tenido hambre.

2. Ojalá **hubiéramos ido** (ir) con ellos al concierto.

3. Me habría alegrado si tú **hubieras venido** (venir) a la fiesta.

4. No creo que ellos **hubieran terminado** (terminar) el proyecto a tiempo.

Exercise 3: Translation Practice

Translate the following sentences into Spanish using the pluperfect subjunctive.

1. If I had known about the meeting, I would have attended.
   Si hubiera sabido de la reunión, habría asistido.

2. I wish they had told me the truth.
   Ojalá me hubieran dicho la verdad.

3. If she had studied more, she would have passed the exam.
   Si ella hubiera estudiado más, habría pasado el examen.

4. I doubt that they had finished before the deadline.
   Dudo que ellos hubieran terminado antes del plazo.

Exercises and Answers

Chapter 6: Subjunctive in Periphrasis

Exercise 1: Conjugation Practice

Conjugate the following verbs in the subjunctive based on the periphrastic construction.

1. *Hacer* (to do) – **Yo quiero que tú hagas**
2. *Venir* (to come) – **Es importante que él venga**
3. *Salir* (to leave) – **Prefiero que nosotros salgamos**
4. *Hablar* (to speak) – **Dudo que ellos hablen**

Exercise 2: Fill in the Blanks

Complete the sentences with the correct form of the subjunctive.

1. Quiero que tú **comas** (comer) antes de salir.
2. Es posible que nosotros **veamos** (ver) una película esta noche.
3. Dudo que ella **haga** (hacer) el trabajo a tiempo.

Exercise 3: Translation Practice

Translate the following sentences into Spanish using periphrastic constructions with the subjunctive.

1. I want you to finish the project before the deadline.
   Quiero que termines el proyecto antes del plazo.
2. It's important that they be on time for the meeting.
   Es importante que ellos lleguen a tiempo para la reunión.
3. I doubt that she can come to the party.
   Dudo que ella pueda venir a la fiesta.
4. We need to leave early so that we don't miss the train.
   Necesitamos salir temprano para que no perdamos el tren.

Exercises and Answers

Chapter 7: The Subjunctive vs. The Indicative

Exercise 1: Identifying the Subjunctive or Indicative

For each sentence below, decide whether the verb in the dependent clause should be in the indicative or subjunctive.

1. **Sé que ella viene** (venir) mañana.
   (Indicative – It's a fact that she is coming.)
2. **Dudo que tú tengas** (tener) razón.
   (Subjunctive – Expresses doubt.)
3. **Es posible que nosotros salgamos** (salir) tarde.
   (Subjunctive – It's a possibility, not certain.)
4. **Estoy seguro de que ellos saben** (saber) la respuesta.
   (Indicative – There's certainty that they know the answer.)
5. **No creo que él haga** (hacer) el trabajo.
   (Subjunctive – Expresses doubt about the action.)

Exercise 2: Fill in the Blanks

Complete the sentences with the correct form of the verb in either the subjunctive or indicative.

1. No pienso que ella **hable** (hablar) con él.
   (Subjunctive – Expresses doubt.)

2. Creo que nosotros **podemos** (poder) hacerlo mañana.
   (Indicative – Expresses certainty.)

3. Es importante que tú **comas** (comer) bien antes del examen.
   (Subjunctive – Expresses importance or recommendation.)

4. Sé que tú **tienes** (tener) razón.
   (Indicative – Expresses certainty.)

5. Dudo que ellos **comprendan** (comprender) la situación.
   (Subjunctive – Expresses doubt.)

Exercise 3: Translation Practice

Translate the following sentences into Spanish, using either the indicative or subjunctive as appropriate.

1. I'm sure that he is coming to the meeting.
   Estoy seguro de que él viene a la reunión.
   (Indicative – Certainty)

2. I doubt that she has finished her homework.
   Dudo que ella haya terminado su tarea.
   (Subjunctive – Doubt)

3. It's possible that we'll go to the park tomorrow.
   Es posible que vayamos al parque mañana.
   (Subjunctive – Possibility)

4. I don't believe that they are telling the truth.
   No creo que ellos estén diciendo la verdad.
   (Subjunctive – Doubt)

5. I'm happy that you are here.
   Me alegra que estés aquí. *(Subjunctive – Emotion)*

Chapter 8: The Subjunctive in Periphrasis Verbal Constructions

Exercise 1: Complete the Sentence with the Subjunctive

Fill in the blanks with the correct subjunctive form of the verb.

1. Dudo que tú **sepas** (saber) la respuesta.
2. No creo que ellos **vengan** (venir) a tiempo.
3. Es posible que nosotros **tengamos** (tener) que esperar.

Exercise 2: Choose the Correct Verb

Fill in the sentence with the appropriate form of the verb in the subjunctive.

1. Me sorprende que tú **hables** (hablar) tan bien español.
2. Temo que él no **pueda** (poder) hacerlo solo.
3. Estoy contento de que ellos **vengan** (venir) a la reunión.

Exercise 3: Expressing Wishes or Desires

Translate the following sentences into Spanish using the subjunctive mood.

1. I hope that you finish the project.
   Espero que termines el proyecto.
2. It's important that they arrive early.
   Es importante que ellos lleguen temprano.

Exercises and Answers

3. I want you to do the homework.
   Quiero que tú hagas la tarea.

Exercise 4: Hypotheticals in the Subjunctive

Complete the following sentences with the correct form of the verb in the subjunctive.

1. Si yo **tuviera** (tener) más tiempo, iría al gimnasio.

2. Es posible que nosotros **veamos** (ver) esa película mañana.

3. Si ellos **fueran** (ser) más responsables, habrían terminado a tiempo.

Exercise 5: Using Subjunctive with Conjunctions

Complete the sentences using the correct form of the subjunctive.

1. Voy a hablar con él antes de que **salga** (salir).

2. Saldré a menos que **deje** (llover).

3. Es importante que nosotros **estudiemos** (estudiar) antes del examen.

Bibliography

As you continue your journey toward mastering the subjunctive and the Spanish language, it's essential to have the right resources to support your learning. Whether you prefer detailed grammar books, interactive online tools, or engaging with authentic Spanish media, the resources you use will play a critical role in reinforcing what you've learned and expanding your understanding. In this section, we'll provide an overview of the types of books, online resources, apps, and media that are most effective for practicing the subjunctive and enhancing your overall Spanish proficiency.

---

1. Comprehensive Spanish Grammar Books

Grammar books are a staple for anyone looking to deeply understand the rules and structures of Spanish. A good grammar book will break down the subjunctive mood in detail, explaining when and why it is used and providing numerous examples of its use in various contexts. These books typically include exercises that allow you to practice conjugating verbs and using the subjunctive correctly. Look for resources that focus on verb tenses, conjugation patterns, and clear explanations of subjunctive triggers such as doubt, emotion, and desire.

---

2. Subjunctive-Specific Guides and Workbooks

If mastering the subjunctive is your primary goal, there are many resources specifically tailored to this area of Spanish grammar. These guides often provide a focused look at the subjunctive mood, explaining its various forms (such as the present, imperfect, and pluperfect subjunctive) and when to use them. Workbooks typically include exercises to reinforce your understanding of these complex forms, offering fill-in-the-blank questions, sentence translation, and multiple-choice tests to ensure you grasp the finer points of subjunctive usage.

---

3. Online Grammar Resources

The internet is a treasure trove of resources for learning Spanish, including detailed lessons on the subjunctive. Online grammar websites often break down each tense and mood with examples, quizzes, and interactive exercises. Many sites offer audio recordings so you can hear native speakers using the subjunctive in real-time, helping you improve both your grammar and listening skills simultaneously. These resources are especially useful for those who prefer learning at their own pace, allowing you to revisit tricky concepts as often as needed.

---

4. Mobile Apps for Language Practice

Mobile apps are a convenient way to practice Spanish wherever you are. Many apps focus on building fluency by providing bite-sized lessons and interactive quizzes that reinforce grammar concepts like the subjunctive. Apps can be a fun way to practice conjugations and sentence structure, often using gamified elements to motivate you. Additionally, some apps feature conversation practice with native speakers or simulations of real-life scenarios where you can apply your knowledge of the subjunctive in context.

5. Podcasts and Video Lessons

Listening to native speakers is an excellent way to familiarize yourself with how the subjunctive is used in everyday speech. Podcasts and video lessons are particularly effective for intermediate to advanced learners who want to see how the subjunctive functions in real conversations. Many podcasts focus on grammar topics, explaining the subjunctive in a clear, engaging way, often with dialogues or interviews to illustrate its use. Video lessons can also break down complex grammatical rules with visual aids, making it easier to understand the nuances of the subjunctive mood.

---

6. Interactive Learning Platforms

If you enjoy learning in real-time, consider using interactive language-learning platforms where you can connect with native speakers or professional tutors. These platforms often allow for personalized lessons focused on your specific needs—whether that's mastering the subjunctive or improving overall fluency. One-on-one tutoring sessions are a great way to practice speaking and writing in the subjunctive while getting immediate feedback and corrections.

7. Spanish Literature, Music, and Film

For a more immersive experience, engaging with authentic Spanish media is one of the best ways to reinforce your language skills. Reading Spanish literature exposes you to rich examples of subjunctive usage, especially in dialogues and descriptive passages. Similarly, watching Spanish films and TV shows or listening to Spanish music helps you internalize how native speakers use the subjunctive in everyday conversations. This type of immersive learning not only improves your understanding of grammar but also enhances your cultural knowledge, making the learning process more engaging and enjoyable.

---

8. Practice Through Writing and Speaking

Beyond structured lessons, one of the most effective ways to master the subjunctive is by applying it in writing and speaking. Journaling in Spanish, focusing on using the subjunctive to express your thoughts, desires, and doubts, will help solidify the mood in your everyday vocabulary. Similarly, practicing conversational Spanish with language partners or tutors gives you real-time opportunities to use the subjunctive naturally. The more you use the subjunctive in actual communication, the more intuitive it will become.

Whether you prefer the structure of grammar books and workbooks or the flexibility of mobile apps and interactive platforms, there are numerous resources available to help you master the subjunctive. The key is consistency—by regularly engaging with these tools and integrating the subjunctive into your daily Spanish practice, you'll find that what once seemed complex will become second nature. Remember, language learning is a gradual process, and the more you expose yourself to different forms of media and practice, the stronger your grasp of the subjunctive and the Spanish language will become.

Good luck, and keep practicing!

Made in the USA
Middletown, DE
18 November 2024